WALKING TO THE ROCKIES WITH MUCKWAH

Volume Three
Schreiber to Vermilion Bay, Ontario

JAMES JOSEPH CAUGHHILL
AKA Homeless James

Other Books by James Joseph Caughhill

Walking to the Rockies with Muckwah Series
Volume 1 – St. Catherines to Sudbury, Ontario – December 2019
Volume 2 – Sudbury to Schreiber, Ontario - March, 2020

***

Layout and Design by Oak Island Publications
oakislandpublications@gmail.com
www.oakislandpublications.com

Published by James Joseph Caughhill
Published in Canada
October 2020

ISBN-13:979-8692406446

The following journal chronicles the amazing adventures of Homeless James and his magnificent malamute Muckwah, as they traverse the treacherous terrain of the great Canadian landscape in the hope of helping other homeless people with pets.

This book is dedicated in memory of my beloved
Baby Girl Muckwah, my personal hero!

CONTENTS

NOTE TO READER

The following is a true account of my walk across Canada with my beloved baby girl and best furry friend Muckwah. All of the names of the people and places have NOT been changed to protect the innocent, because there is none!

Our room at Steve's in Washago, Ontario

CHAPTER ONE

OUR SECOND WINTER BREAK - FIRST WINTER WITH UNCLE STEVE

During our first two weeks back Muckwah and I kept poor old Uncle Steve as busy as a bunny, welfare appointments, fundraisers and making the rounds to visit all of our dear friends in Orillia. Grammy Rose being the very first!

Eventually we were able to settle in to a nice comfortable routine. Steve's dog Dalton was a Paws Canada Therapy Dog, and the two of them would visit local nursing homes three times a week for about four hours per visit. This provided petting therapy for the residents. Steve would just drop us off at whatever one of our fundraising spots was the closest to where they were going that day, then pick us up when they were done. This worked great for the entire winter.

On the third week, James and Jodie Walsh had Steve, Dalton, Muckwah and myself over to their place for a huge spaghetti and meatball dinner. Everyone saved some for Muck. I didn't think that she could eat that much! While we were there James asked if we would like to be on their float again for the Gravenhurst Parade and also for the one in Orillia. After my eyes lit up like a kid on Christmas morning, James just laughed and said: "I guess that means yes!" *You bet your ass it did.*

As you know by now, since visiting my Dad for Christmas back in 2016, I have kept in constant contact with him. We talked on the phone for at least an hour once a week. By the time we took our second winter break, my Dad had moved out of his cramped one room place in Thorold and into a much larger state of the art facility called Linhaven back down in St. Catharine's.

He said that he was so much happier now. They even had a pool table. After I told him how happy this had made my Dad, Steve just up and offered to take us down there for a visit the week before Christmas. We both thought it would make the perfect Christmas present for my Dad.

On November 5, 2017 during my weekly phone call with my Dad, I just up and told him that we would be coming down for a visit. Although the surprise would have been great, for some reason I just didn't want to keep it a surprise. My Dad was just so excited and said that he couldn't wait to see his Baby Girl again, and I said: *"Well what about me?"*

"Oh yeah, you too," He replied. We both got the world's best laugh out of that one, my Dad also told me just how much he had loved the Bald Eagles feather that I had sent him. He had my Aunt Mary get a special frame made up for it. That made me happy. I told him that I loved him. He replied that he loved me too. This was something we always did after every call. Then we hung up. I had absolutely no idea that this would be the very last time that I would ever talk with my Dad!

Just after supper on November 10, 2017 I got a phone call from my little brother Walter. Or Father had passed away from Congestive Heart Failure at 11 o'clock that morning. He was 81 years old. Although it broke my heart and made me cry like a baby, it also came as no surprise. My Dad had been suffering from this condition ever since we lost my Mom, it was the reason that he needed to be in these retirement homes in the first place.

No matter what the doctor said was the official cause of death, I can tell you for a fact that my Dad died from a broken heart. He just didn't want to be here without my Mom. He even used to talk about it all the time. How much he was looking forward to seeing her again. I would always tell him that I wanted him to stick around long enough to see us finish our walk. To which my Dad would say "that it was okay" even if he couldn't, because I had already given him the greatest gift I ever could - I had made him proud of me.

Uncle Steve was the rock that I leaned on through this terrible time in my life. Steve lent me a suit, I got a haircut and shaved my face clean. On November 14, we put Muckwah and Dalton in the back of Steve's car, and my dear Uncle Steve drove me all the way down to St. Catharine's for the service at George Darte Funeral Home. He then took me to St. Vincent De Paul Cemetery, where my Dad was laid to rest with full military honors.

My Dads Military Funeral at St. Vincent De Paul, NOTL

We have a family plot where my Grandfather had purchased plots for my brother and myself, about ten years before we lost my Mom. Not wanting to be "worm food" my older brother Kenny and I had signed our plots over to our parents. This saved my mom and dad about $50 thousand dollars at the time, just because we both preferred cremation.

At least sixty people were in attendance for my father's funeral and I was even able to be a pallbearer. Afterwards, I was able to talk with friends and family that I had not seen in over a year. Everyone was great when most of them congratulated me on finally getting my act together and doing something worthwhile with my life. My Dad had bragged to everybody about my walk across Canada.

All except for my baby brother Michael. That little Asshole tried blaming me for our father's death! WTF? Michael had said that it was all my fault that our dad had gotten sick in the first place and had to go into a home.

Yo Michael you little crybaby bitch. I'm the one who actually stayed in St. Catharine's to help take care of both of our parents. WHERE THE HELL WERE YOU? Oh yeah, I remember. After your girlfriend Wendy gave birth to your second child Corey and started putting on a lot of excess weight that you found unattractive, you decided to abandon her and your two sons in Lewiston New York. Then you ran down to Alabama to shack up with the little southern hottie that you had been cheating with behind Wendy's back! So who has the moral high ground now bitch?

I know that a lot of you think this may have been uncalled for, but compared to what I actually wanted to say, I was actually being kind.

After the funeral, Steve wanted to take a drive up to Niagara Falls to visit the graves of his parents. He then wanted to take a detour through the town of Campton. It was the very first teaching job that he had and was in a one room school house.

This sounded great to me because it would give us a chance to visit our old friend Milo's and his dog Sasha. To explain just who Milo's and Sasha are, I need all of you to hop in to our fictional

DeLorean because we are about to take a ride back to Book One, where I regretfully and sadly forgot to mention dear old Milo's and Sasha. *My Bad.* Anyway, way back in Book One and just after leaving the not so nice town of Grimsby and climbing up Mountain Road to Ridge Road.

Our long walk along Ridge Road took Muckwah and I through the sweet little town of Campton where we stopped at the local variety store. It was the only store in town. This is where I met Milo - the very kind owner of the store. I noticed that he had a dog in the store with him, so I told him that I also had a dog outside. With a big broad smile he said: *"Well don't leave the poor thing out there in this heat, bring her on in!"*

I was a little hesitant at first, but Milo insisted. I brought Muckwah inside and introduced her to Milo and Sasha. My fears were completely unwarranted because our two dogs were instant BFFs. Muckwah and I spent a good two hours with our new friends just talking. We told Milo about what happened to us and what we were now doing about it. Milo was very impressed that I had not only chosen to stand up for myself, but that I had chosen to help others at the same time. Muckwah and I had really loved Milo and Sasha.

Just the look on that sweet old man's face when both Muckwah and I walked into his store for a second time was priceless.

As Steve and I walked into the store with both Muckwah and Dalton, there was good old Milo sitting on the stool behind his counter with Sasha on the floor right beside him. Exactly like we had left them just over a year ago. As he looked up at me, his eyes widened and his face broke into that big broad smile that I remembered.

He then said: *"What are the two of you doing back so soon, thought you were on your way to Vancouver?"*

I told him how my dear friend Steve here had invited us back to Orillia for the winter and about the loss of my dad, Milo looked at Steve and started to say: *"I can't thank you enough for..........wait a minute, I remember you, you were the school teacher here back in the early 60s, you taught my two boys!"*

Well, aint karma something? Steve remembered Milo as well and said: *"I remember you had a dairy farm back then right?"* At that point Muckwah and I may as well have been invisible as Milo and Steve spent the next hour talking about the good old days. I didn't mind one little bit. It made me very happy to see Uncle Steve so happy just chatting with his old friend. On our way back we stopped for supper at our regular McDonalds in Schomberg. This was my third trip back to St. Catharine's with Steve.

With my Dad being gone, I had absolutely no plans for Christmas this year. Steve was going to his sisters but couldn't take Dalton because she was allergic to dogs. This gave me a wonderful idea. I was going to have a fur-ball Christmas! Along with Dalton, Steve had an inside cat named Tommy and fourteen feral cats that he looked after. I set about doing a few extra fundraisers and managed to pick up an 18 lbs turkey, stuffing, mashed potatoes, gravy and cranberries. There was more than enough for myself and all of my little fur buddies.

Just like my Dad had taught me, I put the turkey out to thaw a good twenty-four hours before I needed to put it in the oven. On Christmas morning I completely took over Steve's kitchen. That night I had separate plates of my killer Christmas dinner for myself, Muckwah, Dalton and Tommy. The feral cats got all of the leftovers which was more than the fourteen of them could eat.

This was also the year that Costco opened up in Orillia. It was sometime in March that Steve got his membership. This would start a new tradition that would carry on into the following winter. For a $1.50 you could get a hotdog and a drink. They were the best hotdogs we ever had!

During our first winter with Uncle Steve, I spent a lot of time working on Book One of *Walking to the Rockies with Muckwah*. I had been given a laptop for Christmas. I also helped Steve around the house whenever he needed me. I shoveled a lot of nnow that winter!

I even helped Steve with a few deliveries for his friend Linda who lived in Washago. We collected as well as distributed donations for needy families in and around the City of Orillia. Muckwah and I even stopped in at Pets at Peace North a few times to see our dear friend Sharon who had done such a great job of managing our public Facebook page. Sharon even came out to Steve's to see us a couple of times.

This was how the rest of our break went right up until June 11, 2018 when our dear friend Steve drove us up to the Washago Train Station. I hugged him real hard and I started to cry as we said goodbye. Uncle Steve and I were now so close that he was now exactly like a second father to me. I was really going to miss that old fart!

CHAPTER TWO

TRAIN RIDE TO LONGLAC - ON THE ROAD AGAIN

I had called Karen and Moe about four days before we left just to let Karen know that we were on our way and to make arrangements with Moe to come pick us up. Well wouldn't you know it, as soon as the train pulled into Longlac I looked out the window and there was our dear old buddy Moe standing beside his pickup. It sure feels great to have friends you can count on.

It was a two hour ride back to Karen's where I spent the next five days fixing my cart, airing out my tent, helping Karen with some yard work while Muckwah supervised and swooned over her favorite furry fella Boy.

I now had mobile data with Facebook and Google Earth on my phone. This allowed me to plot my course as we walked. Karen even made arrangements with her friend Jessie who owned a gas bar/variety store in a place called Pays Platt for us to tent beside his store.

Sadly the day came for us to head on down the road. Moe even stopped by to see us off. He took a couple of pictures of Muckwah, Karen and myself beside our cart.

Karen, Muck and I with our cart.

As well as Google Earth, I also had a folding map that showed all of the campgrounds and rest areas. It was even marked for whether or not the rest area had washrooms. About halfway between Schreiber and Pays Platt was one of these rest areas at a place called Rossport. That was where we spent our first night back on the road.

The one thing that gave me a real problem was my excessive weight gain from our eight month winter break. Over the winter I had gone from 190 lbs to 230 lbs. Our first winter break we had both been very active as we had first walked all over Parry Sound and then all over Orillia to do our fund raisers. With absolutely nothing to do in the tiny little town of Washago and Uncle Steve driving us to and from our fundraisers, it had been so very easy to pack on the extra pounds. Walking those first two weeks had been very difficult for both of us, so we tried to keep it to fifteen kilometers per day.

I found us a very nice spot to tent at the Rossport rest area. It was about twenty feet to one side of the washrooms and just about twenty yards from Lake Superior. *My God, what a perfect view.* We had us a few visitors, a great night's sleep and then we were packed up and on the road by 10:00am. Our next stop was the Pays Platt First Nations Reservation, along with Gravel River Provincial Park. It was situated in a valley between two mountains - Rossport and Cavers. I was to later find out that Cavers is the highest mountain in all of Ontario and home to most of the province's Amethyst mines.

It was only 10km to Pays Platt, but it took us all day to get there. Most of the day was spent climbing to the top of Rossport Mountain. It was not all that steep, just very long way to the top. It was 6:00pm by the time we got to the Pays Platt Gas & Variety, so I parked the cart, got my Baby a drink and went inside to meet Jessie. Only Jessie turned out to be Tony - Jessie's Uncle - who was watching the store and had no idea who we were.

After explaining myself, Tony called Jessie on the phone and got things cleared up for us. We found a real nice spot around the back with lots of shade and hydro. Before I could even finish setting up this very kind lady stopped by with two huge plates of supper for the both of us, WOW!

I was once told by one of those sweet ladies back in Shawanaga, that while traveling on any First Nations reservation it didn't matter who you were or what your situation, you will never ever go hungry. That was the understatement of the year. This sweet lady introduced herself as Beverley Goodchild, who later became and still is one of our best friends of all time. It was a Friday night when we got to Pays Platt and to our wonderful surprise.

The next day just happened to be National Aboriginal Day, so Muckwah and I had the extreme privilege of attending our very first Pow Wow.

During the Pow Wow, I was able to have the most amazing conversation with the Tribal Medicine Woman. She explained to me that what I was doing by walking across Canada was something her people called a *vision quest* and that during one of these quests the person was usually accompanied by a Spirit Animal. This would either be a bear, wolf or an eagle - their three most sacred animals. Because Muckwah was 70% Timber Wolf, I was truly blessed by the Great Father because my spirit animal traveled with me in the flesh. It was the coolest thing I had ever been told, but it also sent a freezing cold shiver up my spine.

So we stayed in Pays Platt for two nights and left Sunday morning. Now I had thought that Gravel River was our next stop but I was sadly mistaken. It turned out that we had to get over Cavers first. The climb to the top was so bloody long and steep that we ended up finding a flat spot about halfway up and just tenting there for the night.

It was about 7:00pm the next day when we finally reached Gravel River and Archie's Motel and Coffee Shop. I asked for and got permission to tent for one night off to the side of Archie's. While setting up we had the most wonderful surprise visit from our new friend Beverly and her husband Francis. They invited me into Archie's for some really great spaghetti and Italian sausage. Bev even got a take-out order of the same for Muckwah. My Baby Girl just loved it! Our next night was an uneventful tenting at the side of the highway but the day after that is one for the record books.

As we found ourselves climbing up yet another very, very long hill, we got to the top. On our left was a gravel road with a sign that read *Kama Bay Lookout*. I didn't feel like walking up the very steep gravel road, so we just kept on going. About two killometres later the highway started going down and that's when we came across the most amazing view that I have ever seen in my entire life.

We were now about a good three hundred feet above the level of Lake Superior at the mouth of Kama Bay. There were at least forty islands as far as the eye could see. There was a pullover spot with guardrails so we decided to stop here for lunch. Sadly my cell phone had died and I was not able to take any pictures. *Was I ever pissed about that.* After another very long walk to the bottom we crossed over a bridge with a sign that read *Jack Pine River*. On the other side was a snowplow turnaround with enough room at the one end for us to tent.

Our overnight at Jack Pine River turned into four nights due to a very nasty line of thunderstorms. We were starting to get low on food and water and I was worried that we might run out before the storms stopped. Thanks to being babysat by God, on our second day there a very sweet man stopped by with twenty cans of Holiday Lunch Meat. He saved our butts. He also told me that the river water was safe to drink.

On our last day there we were both eating supper with the tent flap wide open and just watching the rain coming down. I heard something behind our tent but walking around to the front. This turned out to be a 200 lbs Black Bear - what you would call an adolescent. At first this guy scared the crap out of me while Muckwahs ears went back and she bared her teeth. To the utter surprise of both of us this wild bear didn't act mean or aggressive. It was just the opposite. He walked up to the front of our tent and stopped about two feet from us. He then laid down on his belly, looked at my can of lunch meat and gave me the saddest most pathetic look you ever saw.

Although I knew I was being played - I have been played by the best - my heart just melted. This big old fur ball was able to play me for five cans of our lunch meat. The most amazing part of all this is that Muckwah had absolutely no problem with this near being so close to us and me feeding him. I think she knew he was no threat to us. After his fifth can, I showed him my empty hands. He then stood up and walked into the woods. If I didn't know better, I would swear that this was somebody's pet.

After a great night's sleep and our very sweet black bear encounter, we were now on our way to the good sized town of Nipigon. After having to walk all the way around Kama Bay which was an extra twenty-five kilometers. It took us two days to get there, but it was way more than worth it.

Nipigon was one of the friendliest towns we had ever been to. Although they do have the most butt ugly bridge we ever had the misfortune of setting our eyes on. After struggling to keep my lunch where it belonged as we crossed this "eye sore" we took our fist left into town. We then stopped at the first shady tree we could find for our water break.

This just happened to be right beside a brand new tourist lookout that was still under construction. One of the guys working there saw us and came over with six ice cold bottles of water. *What a sweetheart.* I emptied the warm water and put two bottles of the cold into Muckwah's bowl for her. She just loved it! After a really good drink Muckwah lay down and dozed off in the nice shade we now had. Before either of us could even notice a coyote came walking across the road heading right for us. As we both watched in amazement, this wild coyote stopped at Muck's water bowl, drank what was left in it and then just wondered off into the woods leaving both of us with stupid puzzled looks on our faces.

Later when we got into town we met a wonderful girl who managed the towns campground. She gave us a spot free of charge for as long as we needed it. She had been following our Facebook page. We were able to do some fundraisers and I even applied for and got my basic needs check. The one thing I could not find in town was a pair of running shoes in my size. Now that I had my phone charged, I made a post about it on our public page. I got a response from a very kind lady who was going to be driving her sister from Thunder Bay down to Wawa. She got me a brand new pair of size 13 at the Walmart in Thunder Bay and dropped them off on her way. *WOW, what a sweetheart!*

Now, this being July it was very hot during the day, so we were tented beside a very large gazebo that we used for shade and the campground was right beside the town marina. We went swimming every day.

This one time while doing one of our fundraisers we even ran into Bev's husband Francis. He was there to pick up a prescription at the local Pharmacy. I told him where we were tenting and low and behold we just happened to get a visit from Bev the very next day.

Our favorite spot to fundraise was at the Nipigon Library. We had permission. They had a place where I could fill my water jugs and they even let me bring Muckwah inside to cool her off when it got too hot out. They had really good air conditioning. There was even a coffee shop right next door where I would get our morning coffee and a meatball sub that we would share for our supper. While at the library we met a very sweet woman who invited us to spend the night in her very large shed. She lived right beside Black Sturgeon River just the other side of Red Rock and we would be walking right past their house.

To this very day I still miss the sweet town of Nipigon.

Sitting on the dock of the bay in wonderful Nipigon

CHAPTER THREE

SOUTH TO THUNDER BAY?
BECAUSE SOME DUMMY THINKS THEY ARE FUNNY

You would think that you could keep going west from Nipigon - but no - there is no highway, road or even a decent trail going west. If you want to get to Manitoba you first have to go two hundred kilometers south to Thunder Bay and make your way northwest from there. If this was some morons idea of a sick twisted joke, it's really not funny you cheap ass bastards.

Anywho, at first this really pissed me off, but thanks to the Good Lord it actually turned out to be a real blessing. *Go figure.* At this time there was some major highway construction going on just as we got to Red Rock. They were turning Highway 17 into four lanes from Red Rock to Thunder Bay. Separate crews starting at each end and meeting in the middle. With no place to tent at either side, we just tented in the middle between both sets of lanes. *Screw them if they can't take a joke!*

During our next day as we were stopped for our water break this tractor stopped across the road from us and I couldn't help but notice that they were towing a huge plastic cow behind them. It was a man and his wife who invited us over to have some lunch with them. As we ate a wonderful meal of cheese, crackers and kielbasa they told me that they were driving all the way across Canada to raise awareness and support for Canadian Dairy Products. They even left us with a huge piece of homemade Gudas to have for our supper later. Very tragically, I was later to find out that they never made it. Sadly, their rig had been hit by a transport truck somewhere out in Saskatchewan. I actually cried myself to sleep that night. It turned out that the man had been hospitalized while tragically his wife had been killed. To this very day I still have the *Support Milk* button on my safety vest - exactly right where this wonderful woman pinned it.

Our next night however was very nice as we took that sweet woman up on her offer and spent the night in her shed. Not only did this sweetheart put us up for the night, she let me do my laundry and take a shower. She even came out to the shed later with a super huge bowl of homemade stew. There was way more than enough for both of us.

She told me that she and her boyfriend had to go to work real early in the morning and most likely would not be home when we got up. She said I could fill my water jugs from the tap at the front of the house. She then gave me a hug and Muckwah a huge kiss, said goodnight and that was the last time we ever saw her. *Bless you for your kindness my dear.* After packing up and filling my water jugs like I was told to - my Dad always said to never argue with a woman, just do what your told and you just might live longer.

I then checked my map to see what – if any - towns were up ahead of us. There were only five towns for the next 170 km - Hurkett, Dorian, Ouimet, Pass Lake and Crystal Beach. The only store was a Co-op between Hurkett and Dorian. This would be a good eighty kilometer walk, but thankfully I had the foresight to overstock on canned food back in Nipigo. We were now carrying 8-4 liter jugs of water. This night we just tented at another snowplow turnaround and one more the next night. It took us three full and very long days to get to Hurkett but it was well worth the long hot walk.

The very first thing we came across was a huge farm with horses. Muckwah's eyes lit up like a kid on Christmas morning. It was all I could do just to put the brakes on the cart as my Baby Girl literally dragged me over to the fence line. She never barked once, she just stood up on her hind legs with her front paws on the fence and her tail wagging so bloody fast that I was afraid she was going to wag it clean off. To my very pleasant surprise two of the horses came walking right up to her and in the next ten minutes we had five horses at the fence making a fuss over my Baby Girl. We spent at least an hour at the fence until the novelty wore off and we were able to continue down the road. Our next stop was just for a water break where we met a very nice man who said that he was a professional photographer. He asked if he could take some pictures of us, I said: sure, why not. About two months later he emailed me those pictures. I just need to dig way, way back in my emails to find them. Around 5 o'clock that afternoon we finally rolled into the Hurkett Co-Op. We had a great visit with the owner who came outside to make a huge fuss over Muckwah. We resupplied and had us a really great supper of lunch meat and cheddar cheese.

We had a very nice walk to Ouimet where we tented for the night right across from the entrance to the Ouimet Canyon Provincial Park. Our next night we were having the worst time of it just trying to find a place to tent, when we met a wonderful lady out delivering the mail. She told us that her brother lived just two kilometers up the road and that we could tent out front of his place. She was almost done her route and would meet us there. By the time we got there she was standing beside her car in the driveway with her brother beside her. I introduced ourselves, told them what we were doing and why we were doing it. Her brother was very impressed and said we could tent here for a few nights if we needed it. We actually stayed there for two nights, we really needed the break.

Our dear friend Bev actually lived in a town called Jellico (just north of Nipigon) but she worked in Thunder Bay. We got to be babysat by Bev this entire time. She would always stop with something for us and just to make sure we were both okay. Yes, we got adopted again.

Just before Thunder Bay there is a provincial park called Pass Lake and this has a very famous landmark called *The Sleeping Giant*. Right across from the entrance to Pass Lake was a Flying Js truck stop, so we went inside to see if we could tent on the edge of their parking lot. To our wonderful surprise the lady manager just happened to be the mother of the girl who put us up at the campground in Nipigon. *Small world now, ain't it?* She knew all about us, so we ended up tenting there for three days. We had us a very nice spot at the front corner of the lot. She let me bring my phone and DVD player inside to charge them and we had the most wonderful meals from their restaurant. Bev even stopped by with Francis, their daughter Jackie and Jackie's daughter for a long and very great visit.

Now, just before we get into Thunder Bay, I need to backtrack to last winter for a few minutes. During our stay with Uncle Steve I made several new friends on Facebook. Two of them - Karen and Tracie - both lived in Thunder Bay. They both extended invites for us to stay with them when we got there, and we did. We now return you to your regular scheduled reading.

Seeing as how Highway 17 was now fout lanes and very busy, and wanting a more quiet walk we decided to take Lakeshore Drive the rest of the way to Thunder Bay. Our first night was just at the side of the road, but the next day was oh so very, very sweet as we found ourselves at the Crystal Beach Variety Store where we made a great new friend by the name of John.

John owned the store along with half of the laundry mat, pharmacy and restaurant combo next door. He was kind enough to let us tent behind his store and he even ran an extra-long extension cord down to our tent just so we could have hydro. John was such a great guy! Because of a real nasty thunderstorm our one night stay became two nights. That was okay though because I was able to do my laundry, buy some T-1s at the pharmacy and Muckwah and I shared some of the best southern fried chicken ever.

After saying a very sad goodbye to our new friend John we continued on up the road until it started getting dark. That's when we just happened to luck out as we came upon the Lakeshore Variety owned by the most wonderful couple Monika and Emil. We are still very good friends to this day. Monika has become a second grandmother to me. They let us tent at the side of the store and we even had hydro.

The most amazing thing happened at 7 o'clock the next morning. As I was putting my kettle on my portable stove for my morning coffee I heard this very sweet voice ask: *"Are you awake in there, I have something for you?"* As I opened the tent flap I saw Monika standing out front with a tray that had coffee and the most amazing breakfast I ever had in my entire life. Monika's breakfast has never been beat to this very day! Telling you all what Monika made us for breakfast seems to me not to give her the credit she so rightfully deserves, so I'm just going to have to put a picture of it in this book. *You bet your ass I took a picture of it!*

After the world's best breakfast and getting packed up, we were back on the road by 9 o'clock in the morning. Before we left and just after getting a huge hug from our new dear friend Monika, she told me about a place on our way where we could tent for the night called *Wild Goose Beach*. It wasn't too far because we got there just after 5 pm. I got Muck a drink and her supper, set up our tent while she ate and then we went for a walk on the beach. *Holy duck feather's Batman!* This beach was loaded with more Canadian Geese than I have ever seen in one place. Muckwah tried to play with a couple of them and almost got the living crap beat out of her. It looked like swimming was out of the question at least for today so we went back to our tent, rolled out a blanket under a shady tree and settled in for a nice nap. No sooner had I put my head down when I heard a voice say: *"Hey There."*

I sat up to see a man with a Golden Doodle walking towards us, he said: *"Don't worry, this is Sam and he's very friendly with other dogs."* He was curious about us because of the sign on the front of my cart. Sam and Muckwah hit it off right away so I invited him to have a seat with us. If my dog likes you or your dog, then so do I. We talked for over an hour as I told him what had happened to us and what we were doing about it now. Just like me, this man said he had a photographic memory and asked me if it was okay for him to recount our story on his radio station. I was like, *"sure please do, the more people that know about us the better".*

At the time when he said "his radio station" I just assumed he meant the station he worked at. Boy, was I ever wrong! I'm reminded of my Dad telling us that we should never assume anything, because you make an "ass" out of "u" and "me". Nice play on words Pa, but now I think I finally get it!

These words of wisdom hit me like a ton of bricks as the very next day just about two kilometres past *Wild Goose Beach* Muck and I stopped for one of our half hour lunch breaks. All of a sudden a car stopped, and then another and another and so on. Our half hour break turned into three hours as twenty people stopped to see us, they had all heard our story on CBC Thunder Bay Radio. I later found out that the man we had talked with on the beach actually owned that radio station. So very, very cool.

After a three hour break that we wouldn't have missed for all the world, we didn't gain much ground before having to stop for the night. This time we found ourselves at the corner of Lakeshore Drive and Spruce River Road where luckily we were right beside the Shuniah Fire & Emergency Services. Even better, there was a car in the parking lot. I parked Muck and the cart under the only tree there was, got her a drink and went to see if we could tent here for the night. The very sweet girl whom I talked to had also heard our story on the radio and was more than happy to help. She actually laughed out loud when she said: *"at least now I won't have to come looking for you guys."*

As we were heading around back to get set up this pickup truck pulls up beside us and this guy gets out carrying a large McDonalds bag. He introduced himself as Mike Rotteau. He said: *"thought you guys could use some supper."* There was a Big Mac, fries and three cheeseburgers. *WOW!*

Unknown to either of us at the time, Mike was eventually going to be a huge part of my life. You will find out more in Book 4.

Mike told me that he had been out to Ontario for a wrestling match and was on his way home to Saskatchewan when he heard about us on the radio. He decided to stop at McDonalds and then double back on up Lakeshore. *Wow, what a great guy!*

On our next day Lakeshore Dr. became Strathcona Ave. As we were now actually coming into the city of Thunder Bay, and that was where we came across the most dangerous part of our entire walk!

CHAPTER FOUR

TWO WONDERFUL WEEKS IN THUNDER BAY
MUCKWAH GETS TREATED LIKE A QUEEN

Halfway between Strathcona and Thunder Bay the road took an *S* bend and went under a railroad bridge. Right at the first bend, the problem was that there was only enough room under the bridge for the two lanes of road. There were absolutely no shoulders what so ever. When walking the law states that you must walk against the flow of traffic. It's what we normally do but when we got to this bridge it was just too dangerous.

We backed up about thirty yards, dashed across the road, made it up to the bridge and while keeping a constant eye behind us we made a mad dash to the other side. We then stayed in this side for at least another thirty yards before crossing back over. *Scary shit!*

It was August 1 when we finally got into Thunder Bay – Port Athur actually. We had planned to spend our entire time here with Karen out at her place, but she was still on vacation in Switzerland and wouldn't be back until August 6.

I messaged Tracie to see if we could spend a few nights tenting at her place. She said fine but she was going to be leaving for her vacation on the fifth. I then messaged Karen to let her know and dear sweet Karen made arrangements for us to tent for one night with a friend of hers who lived just across the street from her. Now that we were all set we stopped for our break in the shade of the overhang at a Macs Convenience/Gas Bar on Hodder Ave.

We were then going to take Hodder up to Red River Road and that would take us up to Tracie's, but coming out of the Macs we hit a huge pothole that I hadn't seen. The front of our cart hit the ground as my forks folded and my front tire twisted to one side. Luckily, this very nice young lad had seen what had just happened and came running over to help me get our cart off of the road. I did not know what we were going to do, but we still quite a bit of money from all of the donations back in Wild Goose Beach. This nice young man's helped by calling the local taxi company for me. I asked if they had a Handi-Van available and they did.

With the taxi driver holding onto Muckwah, this very nice young man - who actually waited with us until the cab came - helped me roll my cart up the ramp and into the van. *I can never thank him enough!* When we got to Tracie's, the driver parked close to the gate for her backyard. I hooked Muck to the fence and the driver helped me as we rolled my cart into Tracie's yard. I gave him a really good tip. When Tracie got home from work she took Muckwah and I over to Walmart for groceries' and then to Canadian Tire for the brand new tent I had been saving up for.

By the time we got back my phone was charged and Tracie let me hook into her Wi-Fi. I made a post explaining what had happened to our cart and that we were in need of a three wheel jogging stroller to fix it. The very next day a sweet lady from Thunder Bay dropped one off. The day after that our dear sweet friend Beverly stopped by for a visit. She also had a stroller for us. I now had enough parts to fix my cart with spare parts left over for future use.

During this time as I worked on my cart, Muckwah made friends with Tracie's dog and the two other dogs next door. They kept her well entertained and out of my hair. On our fifth day at Tracie's with my cart fixed and all packed up. Seeing as how it was a twenty kilometers walk out to Karen's, Karen messaged her friend who had a cargo van. He came down to Tracie's, picked us up and drove us out to his place where we tented in the back beside his lumber mill.

After a real great night's sleep we took the path he had shown us the day before. Using his Gator he had actually taken us for a ride over to Karen's and back. Karen was home by the time we got there. She gave us a spot to tent with water and hydro and later that day she invited us over to her house for one hell of a great supper.

The next day Karen even drove us into town so I could apply for my basic needs check and because they were so backed up, it was going to take nine days to get it. I did have some money left on me, so on our way back we stopped at Pet Valu where I picked up a brand new leash and collar combo as a belated birthday present. I was not able to afford anything special back in Nipigon.

Our new tent in Tracie's backyard, August 1 2018

We actually only spent our first three night's out in our tent. On our fourth day with Karen and due to a major heat wave - it was 40c plus - Karen insisted that we move into her air-conditioned basement for the rest of our stay. I'm telling you that we just had it so rough in Karen's basement. It was completely renovated and finished living room with 70" flat screen TV, full bar and pool table, two spare bedrooms and a full bath.

Muckwah made great friends with Karen's dog Trooper

Karen even made breakfast and supper for us every single day - although I did have to go outside to smoke. *No big deal.* Karen's friend from across the road came over for coffee every morning, which we all had out on Karen's huge screened in porch off the back of her house. During this entire time I had been in constant phone contact with Bev. I gave her Karen's address and two days later she showed up for a visit. *It was so very sweet of her.*

One of the most amazing things that happened while we were

there is when Karen told me about the Wildwood Variety Store about twenty-two kilometers up Highway 102 and that we would be walking right past it. Karen looked up the number for me and said that I should call and see if I could get permission to tent there. *We did.* On our eighth day with Karen, welfare called to tell me my check was in. Karen drove us back into Thunder Bay to pick up my check and even took us over to Money Mart so I could cash it. We then stopped at Walmart so I could top up on our supplies. That night I got my cart all packed up and put it in Karen's garage. The next day we had very tearful goodbyes as we left the very best place we had ever stayed!

Life is so rough when you're the Queen of all dogs!

Making friends everywhere

If there's one thing to be learned from all of this long distance walking, it's that life can be a real bitch getting back on the road after being off of my feet for fourteen days. First, we had to take Townline to Highway 102 and that would eventually take us to Highway 17 (the Trans Canada). I found this out the hard way as I noticed myself stopping for a break every other kilometer, but the hardest part was when we came to the hill at the end of Townline, it was not a very high hill and only about a quarter of a kilometer long. *But darn, was it ever steep.* It took me a full twenty minutes to shove my cart to the top of that hill, and I almost didn't make it. It took us until 7 o'clock that night to reach Wild Wood Variety where we were already expected. The very nice lady who owned the store came outside to greet us, then showed me where we could tent. While I was setting up, she came back out with two very large bowls of spaghetti and meat sauce

Was it ever great! We had a very nice night, but we both overslept and we didn't get back on the road until 11 o'clock the next morning.

Tenting beside the Wild Wood Variety Store.

We had planned to tent beside the Kam Community Centre, but it started getting dark before we could get there. After crossing over a small river we came across a small empty parking lot right across from a quarry. We tented for the night at the back of the lot. That night we were lulled to sleep by the howling of a wolf pack from way back in the woods. *Boy did we ever miss that sound.* Our next day would take us to a place called Sistonen's Corner's where there was a very huge unmanned Petro Canada Gas Bar designed mostly for tractor trailer trucks. We found a nice out-of-the-way spot and set up for the night.

Just as I was getting set up for the night, this pickup truck pull's in right beside us and these two guys get out to come talk with me. They said that they had heard about us a few weeks ago on the radio, never thought that they would run into us, but so glad that they did. The three of us had a great conversation while they both made the world's biggest fuss over Muckwah and then they both donated $40 to help us out *WOW, what a great couple of guys!* The next morning we were off to a place called Shabaqua Comers, but first we had to go through the big city of Sunshine (population: 26, ha, ha). As we crossed over a river and came into the actual town of Sunshine, we found that the entire town consisted of an out of business lodge and six houses. We stopped for our water break right beside the river and in front of the town sign so I could take a picture. While we were there this very sweet girl named Amanda Sim stopped with some sandwiches and extra water. She worked in Thunder Bay and was on her way home. She lived in the next town up called Finmark which was a very old Finish farming community. She asked where we would be tenting for the night and I told her just at the side of the road.

That night we did find an unused driveway to tent beside and in the morning Amanda stopped on her way to work and asked if we needed anything. I was almost out of my T-1s, so I gave her the money to pick me up a bottle of two hundred. Now our days walk took us up something called Strawberry Hill. It was not steep at all, but this was the longest hill we had ever climbed. Fifteen kilometers long. It took us almost all day, but we kept on going until we got to Shabaqua and the Timberland Motel.

Two great days of rest and relaxation

Seeing as how we had a little extra money, and as I had done absolutely nothing for my fifty-sixth birthday, which was yesterday and it was now August 17 and still very hot out, I decided to rent us a room for two nights. We had been way over spoiled at Karen's. After parking our cart and getting Muckwah her drink, I went inside to get us that room. To my wonderful surprise the manager said that they were expecting us and that a very nice pair of gentlemen had stopped by that very morning, told her all about us and had even paid for a room for us for the night. *WOW!* I then asked her if I could pay for and keep the room for a second night, she told me that would not be a problem.

Our air-conditioned room at the Timberland Motel

After getting our key and parking our cart out front of our room, I started to unload what we would need for two nights. I was unloading that sweet girl Amanda that we had met back in Finmark pulled up right in front of us. As she got out of her car I noticed that she was carrying two bags - one from Shopper's Drug Mart and one from Harvey's.

Amanda had gotten my T-1s as well as three Angus Burgers and fries from Harvey's *Wow, was she ever great!* Our room had two beds and Muckwah started on the floor. After she cooled down, she actually slept all night on the second bed. In the morning we went back over to the Lodge and got coffee and two fried egg breakfast muffins.

There were a bunch of great guys staying in the rooms on either side of us. They were the road crew working on the south side of Highway 17. That night after supper Muckwah and I spent three hours having a few beers and telling our story to these great guys (and girl). Check out time was 11 o'clock in the morning, but we were up at 6 o'clock. We went for our morning walk, had our coffee and muffins. I even stocked up on some extra smokes and we were on our way by 9:30 o'clock that morning.

Hydro Sub Station where we met Fred

CHAPTER FIVE

LONG LONELY WALK TO DRYDEN

After having a real nice relaxing bath the night before, that morning I had emptied and refilled all of our water jugs. The next few towns were going to be very, very far apart – sixty to eightly kilometers. I loaded our cart with as much food and water as we could carry and I still didn't think it was going to be enough. *I was right.* It took us three days to get to the first town of Raith, our first night was just spent at the side of the highway where it took me about an hour's worth of walking back and forth over the tall grass just to flatten it enough to get the tent up. The next night, however we lucked right out and found a fantastic spot with hydro. I was very happy but also very surprised to find something like this out in the middle of absolutely nowhere, this was my first time ever seeing one, I was to later find out that these were hydro sub stations because of the extreme distance between towns out here.

As I was setting up, we had ourselves a visitor. A man in a hydro truck. To my surprise my first thought was not about us getting kicked out. *God Bless Northern Ontario!* As he got out of his truck he walked right up to me, extended his hand in friendship, introduced himself as Fred the local Hydro Manager and said: *"You must be James and this gorgeous creature must be the famous Muckwah. I heard all about you two on the radio a while back and when I stopped at the Timberland this morning, they told me you guys had been there and where now heading north. I hope you don't mind but I picked up a few things and came looking for you."*

Fred had picked up some canned food, extra water and a box of treats for Muckwah. We had a great visit for about an hour with me telling Fred all about our walk while he spoiled the living life out of Muckwah with really great belly rubs. When we had finished talking and just before he left, Fred handed me his card with his name and number on it and said: *"if anyone gives you two a hard time about staying here, you tell them that you have my permission and that they can call me if they want to."*

Darn, was Fred ever a great guy! Now, because it had been so bloody hot out and Fred had only given us a few small bottles of water, by the time we got to Raith, we were down to our last full bottle of water. We decided to take a walk through the town to see if we could find some water. The town of Riath had about fourteen houses - all but one were boarded up. *Holy ghost town Batman!*

We stopped at the only house that had cars in the driveway and signs of life. This was also the Raith Post Office. After knocking on the door several times and getting no answer, we were just about to leave when a car pulled in the driveway. This very kind woman in a nurses uniform gets out and informs me that the lady who lives here is disabled and that she was her personal support worker. She added that normally she would have called the police, but she knew who we were because she was following our Facebook page.

While she went and checked on her client, I got our seven empty jugs and she filled them for us. Because she only came out here three times a week, she told me that this was perfect timing. I couldn't help but laugh when I told her that it was more like divine intervention. She seemed to agree with me when she told me that my faith in God was a very, very good thing. She then gave us both a huge hug and went back inside.

As we left the town of Raith, I couldn't stop thinking about and being down right amazed at the way Muckwah and I were being babysat by God. It really gives a man pause! We now found ourselves on a very long stretch of highway with swamp land on both sides. When we finally found the only patch of dry land big enough to tent on, we ended up having to tent only six feet from the highway. Instead of placing my lights around the tent like I normally did, I spread out our six lights along the side of the highway and on both sides of our tent. I then hung the smaller of my two flashlights from the middle of the overhang outside of the tent. *Safety first.* After two hours of trying to get comfortable on the lumpiest ground we had ever tented on, I finally managed to fall asleep around midnight. We were both woken up by the very bright light from an OPP officer just shortly after 2:00 o'clock. Under normal conditions I would have been very upset, but when I opened the tent flap I couldn't help but start laughing, for standing in front of me was what I can best describe as Ontario's most jolliest OPP Officer.

He was just a little overweight with chubby red cheeks and he was doing his best to stifle his laughter so he could talk to me. When he finally got himself under control, he just looked at me and said: *"there's absolutely nobody back at my division who is going to believe this one."* He then proceeded to tell me that he was responding to a vehicle rollover. I suppose with an overcast sky and absolutely no street lights out here, we could have been mistaken for a rollover. After running my name and finding out who we were, he told me that I had done just the right thing with my lights, said that this was the best laugh he had in weeks and wished us a goodnight.

It took me a very long time to get back to sleep. To this very day, that was the most uncomfortable spot we had ever spent the night at. I didn't wake up until 11 o'clock that morning. I was very stiff and sore with one heck of a backache. Thanks to Amanda I still had plenty of T-1s left. It took us a good three hours before we cleared the marshlands and started seeing real tree's again - one's we could actually use for shade. Just around 4:30 that afternoon we came across another rest stop. This would have been a perfect place to spend the night, but again it was way too early so we just found a shady tree and had us an early supper.

To my pleasant surprise this was also the spot that marked the official change in time zone's. *So very cool.* They also had bathrooms and a real nice picnic area.

While we were there, we even met up with an old friend of ours from the previous summer. It was the same transport truck driver that had stopped to help us on three separate occasions, He informed me that he knew exactly where we were because over the winter he had started a small Facebook page called *Truckers helping Homeless James and Muckwah*. They now had sixty members and had already raised $400 dollars to help us out, which he then handed to me. It was so very comforting to know that we were now being watched over by a great group of long haul truckers. Later we would also find ourselves watched over by several biker gangs. No wonder nobody ever messed with us. Here I thought that I had now just become this big badass, no such luck, but I really was a hell of a lot tougher than I had ever been before!

After such a fantastic supper break, we just walked until it started getting dark when we found a driveway that led up to a closed and locked gate about sixty feet from the highway. Knowing that it was crown land we just found a flat spot off to one side and called it a night. The next day was one of the most amazing days ever and proof positive that God really was looking after us.

We had at least another two days walk until the next town of Upsala and again we were starting to run low on our supplies. This was when we came across an Esso Gas Bar & Restaurant that was supposed to be closed. Just one week before we got there, a very sweet East Indian family - Sukjutt, his wife and two sons - had purchased and reopened the place.

Sukjutt was a very kind man who let us tent behind his place for two nights and even let me use his hydro. As we would find out, Sukjutt was also one of the very best cooks I had ever met. The restaurant was not quite open yet, but every time he made a meal for his family he made extra for us.

While we were there we had a very sweet and surprise visit from the jolly OPP officer we had met that night on the marshlands. His name was John and he had his partner with him whose name was Linda. They had driven by earlier and seen our cart out front, so when they stopped by that night.

Linda had a box of large Milk Bones for Muck and John had two trays of frozen homemade Lasagna for us to share. Sukjutt put them both in his freezer and in the morning, at my request, he thawed one out for our supper. The morning after that he made us a really great breakfast of eggs, bacon, sausage and fried fish. There was plenty for the both of us. Muckwah and I really loved our stay with Sukjutt and his family.

Me, Muckwah and Sukjutt in front of our Tent

Sukjutt's Esso, Variety Store & Restaurant

This time, after a very, great night's sleep, we were up, packed and on the road by 9:00 o'clock in the morning. It was twenty kilometers to Upsala and I wanted to do it in one day. After a long but very nice walk - it had finally cooled down some - we stopped in at the very first store we came to. I was almost out of smokes but sadly the XTR Gas Bar/Variety Store didn't carry any because most of their counter staff were under eighteen years old. The grocery Store up the street did, so as we got to the grocery store I noticed a huge backyard behind the store. After buying a carton of smokes because we had no idea how long until our next store, I asked if I could tent for the night behind her store. She then asked me if I were by myself, and when I told her that I had a dog with me, she told me that regretfully she couldn't help us. She had a dog that didn't get along with other dogs at all, but she then called her friend who owned the XTR Gas Bar and got us permission to tent there for the night. Due to a nasty thunderstorm, our one night turned into two nights.

This actually turned out to be freaking fantastic because we not only had a great spot with hydro, but the very next day as I was talking with Uncle Steve on the phone and he was telling me about his niece and her daughter who were in the area and keeping an eye out for us, this nice lady walks up to me and says: *"excuse the interruption, but you wouldn't be James would you?"*

I was like: *"why yes, yes I am."* She then said that her uncle back in Washago had told her all about us, where we were and that she should keep an eye out for us. I couldn't help but start laughing as I told her: *"you must mean you're Uncle Steve, the guy I'm on the phone with right now."* The look on her face was priceless!

Two wonderful days at the XTR Gas Bar in Upsala

I then handed her my phone so her and her daughter could talk with Uncle Steve for a bit. After getting my phone back they both introduced themselves and told me that they had picked up a few things for us on their way through Dryden. There was lots of canned goods and eight brand new jugs of water. This was great because the jugs I had were the ones I had gotten way back in Sault Ste Marie and they were getting real beat up and old.

Steve's niece asked if we had eaten supper yet, and when I told her that we had not, she said that supper was on them. They then went into the restaurant and in twenty minutes they were back with three large orders of mild chicken wings with garlic bread. *WOW!*

We ate at the picnic table beside my tent with all three of us tossing chicken to Muckwah. In total we must have spent at least two hours together when the girls said that they wanted to get back on the road so they could make their motel room before dark. They were staying at the Timberland Motel, funny old world now isn't it. They both got a good laugh when I told them that we had just stayed there a few nights ago. Muckwah and I had us a very great but also very busy day. With full tummy's and after taking Muck out to the field behind us so she could do her business, we both just crawled in to our tent and called it a night. No sooner than my head had hit my pillow I saw red and blue flashing lights from a police car that was parked directly in front of our tent, I thought to myself: *Oh Shit, what now?*

But as I opened the tent flap, there was good old John sitting on the hood of his cruiser and laughing his ass off. I couldn't help but start laughing myself as I told John: *"I suppose you think that was funny."* John was like: *"yeah I do."*

John then turned to Linda who was sitting in the passenger's seat and loudly said: *"I think we have their attention girl, you can turn them off now."*

Linda then got out of the car with a huge grin on her face and a large plastic bag in one hand. She then looked at John and said: *"this was all his idea."*

I told her not to worry because I had gotten a big kick out of it. As I stepped out of the tent bringing Muckwah with me they both came up to the tent to say hi and make a huge fuss over my baby girl. Linda then handed me the bag she was carrying, it was full of dog treats,

Our next town was called English River and was a good three day walk from Upsala. Our first night was spent tenting beside a small power station in between the highway and the railway tracks. On our next day just around noon and just before we were about to climb a hill that went over those tracks. We were stopped for a water break when we got a very nice visit from some of the road crew guys whom we had met back at the Timberland. They told me that they were doing a job out in a town called Ignace and were on their way back to Thunder Bay to pick up some extra equipment. They then told me that they would be coming right back this way in the morning and asked me if we needed anything. I told them that we had been very well supplied but that I was getting very low on my Tylenol 1's. The driver said that he would see what he could do. Just after we got over the tracks and down the other side, up in front of us the road took a huge bend to the left. We got closer to the bend amd I noticed a small lake on our left. Behind the lake was about a half dozen run down and boarded up cottages (looked like an out of business campground.

Sure enough, as we got around the curve, there on our left was an overgrown driveway with just enough room on the one side for our tent. After getting the tent up and just as I was setting up our lights we had another visit from yet another old friend. *Stalker alert! Just kidding.* It was the same sweet man who had dropped off all of that canned lunch meat for us way back at Jack Pine River. He handed me a receipt and said that he had rented us a room for one night at the English River Motel. *WOW, what a sweetheart!* The next morning we had only walked about three kilometers when our friends from the road crew pulled off to the shoulder across from us and the driver got out, came over and handed me a bottle of 200 Tylenol 1's. The people of northern Ontario were the very, very best! From where we had tented it was only about fifteen kilometers to English River. It was a very hot day so we just took our time and many water breaks. Muckwah even enjoyed some play when we found a spot with very tall grass and lots of shade.

We got in to town about 5 o'clock, and stopped a kilometer short of our motel for one of our breaks after I spotted a huge bush just filled with ripe wild blueberries. Yes, I made a pig of myself. For the record, English River was a very tiny town with about six houses, two motels – one out of business – and an out of business gas station. Good thing we had stocked up back in Upsala. After walking around an S-bend in the road, we finally came to the English River Inn. After checking in and getting what we needed for the night out of our cart, I left Muckwah in the air-conditioned room while I went over to the little store they had and got us about ten Hot Pocket's to share for our supper. When I got back Muckwah was sound asleep.

Playtime

I felt so bad having to wake the poor girl up, but I really wanted her to eat something. It was well worth it because she actually ate seven of the ten Hot Pocket's. I ended up having to go back for a few more. That night we had us one of our best restful sleeps ever. We got up at six in the morning, but the little store wasn't open until seven so we took a walk down by the small lake that they had.

I got to take a picture of Muckwah sitting on her second Dock of the Bay. *Great Otis Redding song, Batman!* To our wonderful surprise, the sweet lady who owned the Inn with her husband had actually made fresh waffles and pancakes for breakfast. I got an order of both for each of us. As I was checking out, the very nice owner told me that there was a rest area just fifteen kilometers further up the road and that we would be able to tent there.

Stopped for a photo-op on our way out of town

We only spent the one night in English River, but it was one of the best nights we ever had!

On our way out of town, we came to a bridge that crossed over the actual river with a big sign that read English River. *Holy Photo Op, Batman!* After a real nice days walk we got to the rest area about four o'clock in the evening, set up, took a walk around the park that was the rest area. Then we got us something to eat and called it a night. Our next night was just spent at the side of the road where we had a very nice visit with a local couple, Heather and Don. They'd been keeping an eye out for us. Apparently our fame had gotten way ahead of us and we were not only expected in Ignace but Dryden as well. We had a TV interview waiting for us in Dryden. We also had a Fan Club waiting for us in Ignace of about thirty people.

Heather gave me her cell number and said to call when we got close to town. She had a special meet and greet set up for us at someplace called Tower Hill, so I promised her that I would.

We were still twenty-five kilometers Ignace and I wanted to get there in one day. Muck and I were up at five o'clock in th rmoning and on the road by six. We didn't get to Tower Hill until seven in the evening.

I called Heather around six o'clock that night like I said I would. When we finally got there, there was ten people waiting for us including the town's Mayor. *WOW!* Heather took a whole bunch of pictures, and informed me that they had gotten together and rented us a room at the local motel for two nights. When we were all settled in, I was to come down to the restaurant for supper. After getting settled in, I took Muckwah for her nighty walk, put her in the air-conditioned room with the TV on to keep her company and went downstairs for supper. *WOW what a supper it was!* I had a double order of spaghetti snd meatballs with way more than enough left over for my baby girl along with cake and ice cream for desert. All of the people I had met up on Tower Hill were at the supper with me. Including some children and grandchildren. We talked some during supper and for about an hour afterwards. The Mayor asked me if I wouldn't mind coming to their church the following afternoon for a BBQ and maybe to say a few words about our walk. I was more than happy to accept.

The Motel we stayed at in Ignace

When Muckwah and I got to the church that following day, I was so very surprised to find out that this BBQ was actually in our honor. I was the main speaker and about forty people showed up. Seeing as how Muckwah is my favorite subject, I must have babbled on for at least an hour and a half. When I had finished and as we all sat down to eat, there must have been at least fifteen kids gathered around us asking all sorts of questions and making a huge fuss over Muckwah. I felt just a little overwhelmed.

Before continuing on to Dryden, I do need to back this story up just a little bit - it's sort of important.

After leaving that rest area, we had stayed at our first night after English River and just before we came to the spot where we met Heather and Don, Muckwah and I were on our way down one of the multitude of hills in Ontario when a man on a Harley stopped across from us. He parked his bike on the shoulder, walked over and introduced himself as Gary Woods. He said: *but you can just call me Woody, everybody does."*

Woody told me that he was on his way home to Dryden, that he had just come from the Harley Dealership in Thunder Bay.

After having to get his Fairing replaced, he had seen us two days ago when he was on his way there. Regretfully, he didn't have the time to stop. While getting his bike worked on, Woody just happened to mention seeing a homeless guy with a huge husky pushing a cart west towards Ignace. Something you didn't see too much of in the middle of nowhere!

Woody told me that the guy he was talking with just looked at him kind of funny and said: *"You mean that you haven't heard of the guy walking across Canada with his dog, Damn Dude, those two came through here just over a month ago, they were all over the News and the talk of the town for several weeks."*

Woody said that after hearing our story he decided to make a point of keeping an eye out for us on his way back. After a very nice talk with Woody, he handed me a fifty dollar bill to help us out and invited us to spend a few days with him and his family when we got to Dryden. He then gave me his address and phone number.

Those few days actually turned into eight days as I applied for, received and then had to wait for my basic needs check.

Muck with her new BFF Hazley playing in Woody's yard

The World's Sweetest Bed Thieves, Woody's Garage

CHAPTER SIX

DRYDEN TO VERMILLION BAY –
IT'S GETTING COLD OUT

We now return our story to Ignace, Ontario. After a great BBQ, we headed back to the motel where we met up with our old friends from the road crew. They informed me that they were currently blasting rock between Ignace and Dryden and that it would be way too dangerous for us to try and walk the highway for the next week or so. I called Heather and told her the bad news we had just gotten. She said that Don would be more than happy to come pick us up in the morning and drive us all the way in to Dryden. *WOW, are these guys ever great!* After a great breakfast - double meat for Muckwah, as always - Don helped me load our cart and belongings into the back of his pickup. I got Muckwah up and into the back seat and we were now on our way to Woody's house in Dryden. I try my very best not to accept any rides. it feels a little like cheating - but when it comes to our safety, I really don't have any other choice.

I had called Woody the night before to let him know that we were getting a ride out to his place. He said that was great and he would keep an eye out for us. When we got to Woody's the first thing I noticed is that his yard was completely fenced in. Muckwah was going to love it here. As Woody helped Don unload my stuff from the truck, Woody said that I should introduce Muckwah to his daughter's white husky, Hazley. After many butt sniffs, Muckwah and Hazley broke into full play mode. They were instant BFFs right from the start. As the two girls romped it up in the back yard, I went over to Woody's garage where he had a place for us all set up. Woody had a double door two car garage with all his tools and his two Harley's on the one side. The other side was his "man cave" with a couch, chairs including an old barber's chair he was restoring. There was a full size fridge, stereo system and even a 70" flat screen TV. *WOW!*

After unpacking and getting all set up, I told Woody that I wanted to take a walk over to the welfare office to apply for my basic needs check. It was only five blocks away. Since it t might take more than a few days to get one, Woody was so sweet that he told me we were welcome to his garage as long as we needed it. When we got there, I found a spot to hook up Muckwah, went inside to apply. When I walked up to the counter and gave them my name, the girl behind the counter looked at me and asked: *"Where's Muckwah at?"*

When I told her that I left Muckwah outside, she said: *"Why would you do a silly thing like that, we've all been looking forward to meeting your baby girl."* The look of surprise on my face must have given me away because this girl just started to laugh and told me that it was her sister that had taken care of me back in Thunder Bay. She had told her everything about us and that we would be coming through Dryden. After bringing Muckwah inside, the entire staff came out to the lobby to make a fuss over her. *So very, very sweet!*

While at Woody's, I had a shower. His very kind wife washed my clothes for me but her machine wasn't big enough for my bedding, so Woody drove me over to the coin laundry where they had the large machine's. On our second day at Woody's, Woody and his wife were having their coffee in the living room. While I was talking with Uncle Steve out in the kitchen, when all of a sudden I heard Hazley crying and screaming like she was being attacked by something. As I looked out the screen door, I saw Hazley in a panic as she was frantically struggling to get her head up from the back deck. She was wearing a choker chain that had gotten stuck between two boards. In one single motion I dropped my phone, yelled at the top of my lungs: *"Woody, get the hell out here now!"* He ran out the back door and forced Hazley's head as close to the deck as I could. I then yelled at Woody: *"Get something to cut this damn chain right now.*" Woody didn't even hesitate and in less than a minute he was back with bolt cutters. I held Hazley as still as I could and Woody got the chain cut on the first try, When we got her free, her eyes were bloodshot and swollen, but she was alive. The poor girl had been literally thirty seconds away from choking to death! After making sure Hazley was okay, we just sat there looking at each other for at least ten minutes.

When either of us finally spoke, it was me first, and even as the words were coming out of my mouth, I was truly amazed at what I was saying, it went something like this: "*Act of God dude, act of God.*" When Woody asked what I meant, I just said: "*Think about it, you and me meeting. You inviting us out to your place, you do realize that it was for this reason. Didn't God just have the two of us together in the exact spot and at the exact time he needed us? You do know that God put us together to save that dog's life.*"

I will never forget that warm puzzled look on Woody's face as the tears started to roll down his cheeks. That afternoon Muck and I took a walk over to the local pet store where I purchased a proper collar for Hazley. It was a real pretty pink one. To this very day, I still carry what's left of Hazley's choker chain.

The next day while Woody was out and his wife and daughter were at work - they had left the house open for me just in case I needed anything - I was sitting on the back porch with Muckwah and Hazley curled up at my feet. This very nice young man came to the gate and introduced himself as Woody's friend Tommy Johnson.

Tommy was a reporter for the local TV Station, Shaw TV and he wanted to know if he could do an interview with us for his network. I told him that we would love to and then invited him in the yard for a chat. Sadly, Tommy was very busy and had to decline, but asked if he could come back the next day with his equipment. I told him sure why not. You can find this interview if you Google *Homeless James and Muckwah.* I have to mention the three times Woody took me to his favorite restaurant *The Patricia Inn* on Government Road. It's funny because the first time he asked me if I wanted to get something to eat with him, I said: "*Sure, you guys got a KFC or Taco Bell in town?*"

Woody just looked at me and said: "*Who in the hell eats that crap?*" Apparently me, Taco Bell's Mexi-Melts are my all-time favorite! Well, Woody was right, the food at Patricia's was to die for. While I was in

Dryden, we went there two times for supper and once for lunch. Woody had great taste in restaurants.

On our fourth day in Dryden, Tommy showed up at ten o'clock in the morning with his camera and microphone. We did what is still my favorite interview. Tommy gave me his card and asked me to call him when we were ready to get back on the road, because he wanted to film some footage of us actually walking. He was such a sweet guy and Muckwah and I really enjoyed the time we spent with him.

While in town Muck and I stopped by the local IDA Pharmacy to pick up some T-1s. The elderly gentleman who was the pharmacist also owned the store. He was such a sweet kind man that we came back three more times just to talk with him.

Sadly and like always the day came when my cheque was in and we no longer needed to stay in Dryden. This is the one and only part of our walk that I really hate. This time was extra sad because I had to part Muckwah from her new best play pal Hazley. This made me cry. I had absolutely no idea that we would be back to visit them twice before we stopped for the winter.

The day before we left I walked Muck over to pick up my cheque. While her and Hazley played in the yard, Woody took me to Money Mart to cash it, over to Walmart for my supplies and then to Patricia's for my third and final time. I spent that night packing and after coffee and muffins with Woody and Hazley. We were on our way by ten in the morning. I called Tommy to let him know and he told me that he would catch up with us in an hour or so.

Something I had not noticed on our way in to town the first time because Don's truck had A/C and we had the windows up was the smell. As we started walking out of town, the smell became almost unbearable. Dryden had a paper mill and they dumped all of their toxic waste into a canal fed from the river. This consisted of the chemical's used to bleach the paper white. It took over an hour to get that stupid smell out of my nose.

Tommy caught up with us during our second water break. He did a great job filming and I talked as we walked.

Our next town was a sweet little place called Oxdrift, which was way more than a day's walk away. As we were having one of our breaks this nice man stopped to see us. He told me that his wife was following our Facebook page and invited us to tent beside their trailer for the night. They were just up the road at a place called

Robin Court in Lot #11. We took them up on the offer and had a great night's sleep. They even let me use their hydro. In the morning we were on our way to Oxdrift.

When we got there we stopped for a break at the Oxdrift Country Store and the nice lady who worked there even agreed to come out and take a picture of us. Oxdrift boasted Ontario's largest sheep farm and store called Egli's Sheep Farm. As we passed the sheep farm it started getting dark and we needed a place to tent for the night. Along the way we passed a church that looked like it had not been used in about forty years. We were thinking about tenting there, but the church was all boarded up, the gates chained and locked and they had *No Trespassing* signs all over the place. It was definitely not user friendly!

We did however finally find us a spot. It was dark by time we found it but lucky for us not only was this spot on the same side as us. It was a brand new thirty foot digital sign for the sheep farm, that lit up the entire area with more than enough room for our tent. It even had a hydro plug that worked! *It's just great being babysat by God!*

It was now the last week of September and the nights were getting very, very cold. I had been using my space heater since leaving Dryden. In the morning as I was packing up this car stopped beside us and this very sweet girl got out and handed me a pair of sandwiches. She introduced herself as Veronica and told me that she lived with her Dad just north of the next town called Vermilion Bay.

Veronica was on her way to Dryden for a doctor's appointment. She told me that between here and Vermilion Bay there was a variety store called Eagle Junction and that they should let us tent there and we would also have hydro.

Veronica was as helpful as she was sweet. Now Muckwah and I were on our way to Eagle Junction.

The days were now getting real short, leaving not much walking time. For the second time, we didn't get to where we were going until after dark. It was already 7:30 pm by the time we got to Eagle Junction. The place was already closed for the night. Not having any other choice we found a spot at the side of the store, set up my tent in the dark and then found an outside plug so we could have heat.

Me and Muckwah the Oxdrift Country Store

Muck and I had supper and went to bed. About two o'clock in the morning, I woke up freezing my ass off. Our heater had stopped working. After checking to make sure the cords were both plugged in, I finally determined that our heater had overloaded their breaker. The ice machine wasn't working either.

I went back to the tent, pulled Muckwah right up beside me and pulled the two comforters over the both of us. That did the trick and I was able to finish the night with a warm sleep. In the morning we were woken up by a man tapping on my tent and saying *"hey in there."* When I opened the flap to ask him what he wanted, he told me that the lady inside would like to know what we thought we were doing camping beside her store.

I wasn't camping, I was tenting you dumb shit. I didn't tell him that. Instead, I went inside to talk to this lady. As soon as I told her who we were she just looked at me wide eyed and said: *"I'm so very sorry about that, I had no idea it was you and Muckwah.* I told her not to worry and that it was my fault because we got here too late to ask permission.

I then told her about accidentally tripping her breaker with my heater. She didn't seem to have a problem with that. *She was just such a sweetheart.* She invited me for coffee and a muffin and asked if I could go get Muckwah and bring her in so she could say hello to my baby girl. She had a Malamute of her own – it was only an eight week old puppy. Muckwah just loved the puppy and was so gentle with the sweet little thing.

We didn't spend a whole lot of time at Eagle Junction, but our time there will never be forgotten. We were a little late getting back on the road, but that didn't matter because we were now only ten kilometers from Vermilion Bay. As we were about to leave the parking lot, a car stopped beside us and this lady gets out with this excited look on her face. After telling me just how happy she was to have found us, she informed me that her husband and a couple of his friends had gotten together and rented us a motel room at the Pine Grove Motel, just before you get into town. Her sister lived in Dryden had told her all about us and she was now following our Facebook page.

We had stopped for our first water break just after walking across the Eagle River. While there our new friend Veronica stopped to see us with her dad Raymond. There was some major snow in the forecast and they wanted to invite us to come and stay with them for a bit. I told Veronica about the room we already had for tonight, but we would be more than happy to take their offer in the morning. Veronica informed me that they lived quite a ways out of town – about thirty kilometers north to be exact, at a place called Big Canyon Lake. They had a good size utility trailer and would be happy to come pick us up around ten o'clock in the morning. I told her that sounded great and we were looking forward to it.

Before leaving, Veronica told me that they were now on their way into Dryden. She had a prescription to pick up and asked if there was anything she could get us for supper. I jokingly said: *"may be a small bucket of KFC."* She said not a problem, gave us both a hug and was on her way. Muck and I stopped for two more water breaks before Vermilion Bay.

Just about two kilometers before town, Veronica stopped right beside us. She rolled down her window and handed me our bucket of KFC, then said they would see us in the morning. *Wow, what a sweetheart this girl was.*

Now during this walk, Muckwah and I have met so many fantastic people, but the sweet kind hearted woman who managed the Pine Grove shot right to the top of the list. Right beside Monika from the Lakeshore Variety. I must have chatted with her for over an hour as we were checking in. She came outside to make a fuss over Muckwah and she even showed us to our room. About an hour after we got settled in, I heard a knock at our door. It was our sweet motel manager with a huge bowl of homemade stew. She said: *"thought you two might be hungry."* I didn't have the heart to tell her that we had just devoured a bucket of KFC. After I accepted her kindness, Muck and I just made pig's out of ourselves because we never let homemade stew go to waste! It didn't take long to fall asleep with our bellies that full.

In the morning when Veronica and Raymond showed up, we were all packed and ready. After stopping at a place called Quacker's Diner for breakfast and at another place called Bobby's Corners for gas, we then headed straight north on Blue Lake Road.

Our room at the Pine Grove Motel

Our last stop of 2018 – Vermilion Bay

CHAPTER SEVEN

OUR REALLY GREAT STAY IN VERMILION BAY

For some reason I expected to be staying in a cottage, but to my surprise Veronica and Raymond had a very good size two story house all the way out here. There were a dozen more cottage's up and down the lake that they looked after during the off-season. They even had a spare room for Muckwah and I to use.

After unloading our cart, unpacking what I thought we would need, Raymond told me that I could store my cart in the garage next door to them. The people who lived there were very good friends and wouldn't be back up here until the spring.

Veronica and Raymond even had a pair of very friendly dogs named Winston and Anchor. They both became instant BFFs with Muckwah. After getting my room all set up, Veronica wanted to take us for a walk and show us around the place. *My God!* This was one of the most amazing places we had ever been to. No wonder they loved living up here. Great Canyon Lake was just about the most beautiful and crystal clear lake we had ever seen. They had their own dock on a very nice beach and they had a small fourteen foot boat as well, as a really nice pontoon boat tied up to the dock. Veronica offered to take us for a ride later.

It was now the beginning of October and the snow comes very early up here. This put an end to our walking for the year, so during a really, really kick ass supper that night Veronica told me that after talking it over with her Dad, they both wanted to invite us to spend the winter out here with them. Getting my welfare would not be a problem. Raymond was on the Dryden Board of Directors.

We happily accepted the invitation.

Veronica said that she had to go back in to Dryden in the next few days and she would be more than happy to take us with her so I could apply for full benefits. I had absolutely no phone signal out here, but fortunately they did have a land line. Later that night I called Uncle Steve to give him the great news and tell him exactly where we were. As we were talking Steve sounded a little disappointed that we would be staying up here for the winter. When I asked what was wrong, Steve told me that he had just put his house up for sale and that he was hoping we could come back to Washago for one more winter because he could really use my help. After everything our dear beloved Uncle Steve had done for us, this was a no brainer. I told Steve that I would call Via Rail and get us on the very first train back to Washago!

When I broke the news to Veronica and Raymond, they were both so very understanding and said we could stay here as long as we needed. They added that they would be happy to babysit Fred - our cart - for the winter. Raymond even told me that Via Rail actually stopped only fifteen kilometers from here at a place called Macintosh Crossing. He offered to drop us off and then pick us up in the spring.

We would have loved to have spent the winter up here, but now we were both really looking forward to going home to Washago and Orillia one more time. Muckwah and I had fallen in love with both of those towns and we had every intention of settling down there when we finished our walk. After making our reservations for fourteen days from now. We now needed to find a large pet carrier that I could use to take Muckwah on the train with me.

Veronica was so sweet that she let me hook into her WiFi. I made a post asking for help and in four days we had our pet carrier. It took most of the money we had left to pay for our tickets. I ended up taking Veronica up on her offer to take us to welfare. When we were in Dryden I had gotten a check for September and I was still eligible for Octobers check. On our third day there I got Muckwah in to the back seat of Veronica's car and we were off to Dryden.

The look on Woody's face when Muckwah and I walked into his backyard and knocked on his door was priceless. Even better was the reaction from Hazley. I got one quick lick and then it was off to full play mode with Muckwah. Those two really missed each other. We had gone to welfare first and then Veronica dropped us off at Woody's so we could visit while she was at the doctors,

While waiting for our train we had the time of our lives at Canyon Lake. I also helped out around the place quite a bit. I helped Veronica clean out their huge barn so she could get access to their bulldozer for the winter. *Yes, they actually owned a bulldozer!* I even got to meet Veronica's big brother Richard after Veronica threw one of the tracks on the bulldozer as she was clearing some trees and shrubs on one of their many trails. Richard was the only one who knew how to get the track back on properly. Raymond and I went with them in case they needed our help - they did. During this entire time Richard and I had the time of our lives teasing Veronica about what a lousy bulldozer driver she was. She had just as much fun with that as we did.

The one day when they both had to go into Kenora, they asked if we wanted to go with them for the ride. I agreed. This would give us a chance to see what we would be walking through come spring. After we stopped at the Chrysler/Jeep dealership to pick up a part for Ray's truck, they took us to the most wonderful restaurant for lunch. It was called Yesterday's Restaurant. We left Muckwah to sleep on the back seat of the truck with the windows open while we all went in for lunch.

Muckwah's very first boat ride on Big Canyon Lake

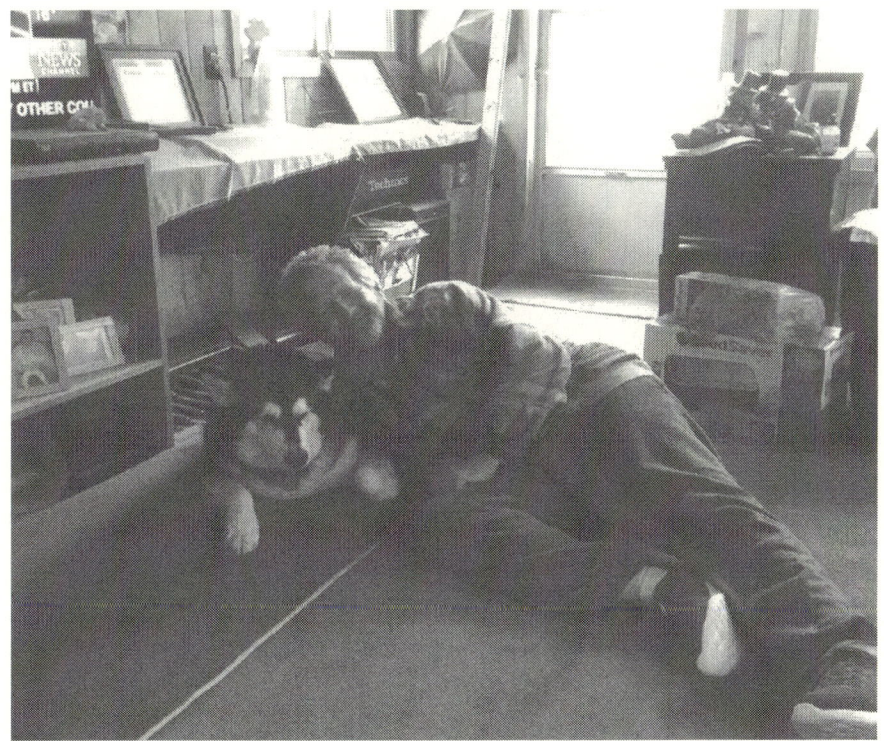

Relaxing with Daddy at Veronica's and Ray's place

I ordered a Club sandwich with fries and it was so good but also so bloody big that Muckwah ended up with half of it. We both managed to keep busy and Veronica and Ray were a great help with that. They took us to Quacker's two more times and when my check was ready, Veronica took us back to Dryden so I could pick it up and cash it. She even took us shopping at Walmart. The very best part of that trip was when we stopped in for a visit at Eagle Junction on the way back. Of course Veronica and Ray were good friends with the owner. *You just have to love these small towns.* Our dear friend at the store said that she was so very happy for us and that we could not be in better hands. Her puppy was just thrilled to see Muckwah again.

They even took us in to Kenora two more times including lunch. The time I do need to mention is when Muck and I went with just Raymond in his truck. He had a Dodge 1500 with a Hemi. Ray said that he wanted to show me their back road shortcut. It was a single dirt lane called Gorden Lake Road.

For me, this turned out to be the shortcut from hell. The funny guy that Ray was, I should have known he was doing this on purpose. This road was nothing but hill's and curves and Raymond was going anywhere from 80-100 kilometers per hour. *He knew exactly what he was doing!* The worst part came as we were going up a steep hill and Ray just floored it. As we hit the top of the hill it went right back down even steeper with a ninety degree curve at the bottom. Scared the living life out of me. Shortly after that curve the road finally and thankfully came to an end. I looked over at Ray, who was now laughing his head off as he asked: *"now wasn't that fun?"* I told him: *"Yeah, loads, just like what I now have in my shorts."* We both burst out laughing. Best roller-coaster ride ever.

One other thing I do want to mention is just what great cooks both of them were. Every morning Ray would make bacon, eggs and toast, farm fresh eggs, really thick farm fresh bacon and homemade bread for the toast. Winston and Anchor always shared the bacon grease and I always saved a little for my baby girl. Then Veronica always did supper, and she'd BBQ whenever she could. With every meal Veronica would make the very best scalloped potatoes I ever had in my entire life!

CHAPTER EIGHT

BACK TO WASHAGO –
OUR SECOND WINTER WITH UNCLE STEVE

S adly the time came for us to catch our train. I wasn't in tears this time because I knew that we would be back in the spring. Our train didn't get there until two o'clock so I waited until after breakfast to pack up. I took Muckwah for one more walk down to the beach. We then piled all of our stuff in the back of Ray's truck and headed down to catch our train.

The last time we caught a train from up north here it was ten hours late. This dummy was actually fifteen minutes early and we almost missed it. The last time it was a thirty-three hour ride to Washago. This time it took us two and a half days. It was our third time so we were well prepared with lots of water and food.

Something strange that I noticed during our several get off and stretch your legs stops, was the hard time Muckwah was having getting back up on the train. I had to help her every time. I just put it down to eating way too well and being off our feet for fourteen days.

When we finally got to Washago, dear old Uncle Steve and Dalton were sitting in the parking lot waiting for us. My God, were we ever happy to be home.

After getting unpacked, Steve took us into Orillia so I could apply for my full benefits. We then stopped in to visit Grammy Rose and finally stopped at Arby's for supper. The next day Steve took us shopping at Walmart and we then went to the Hock Shop where I picked up a second hand 36" flat screen TV.

While we had been gone Steve had made a new friend his own age named Jackie Taylor. I used to tease him about having a girlfriend. When Muckwah and I arrived back in Washago, Steve and Jackie had already started sorting things out for the move. I helped were and when I could by doing most of the heavy lifting.

It wasn't until sometime in early November that I discovered Muckwah had a hard lump in her belly and she was getting small lumps on her skin. Right away I made an appointment with Steve's vet. After her exam the vet told me that Muckwah had Swollen Piametria. This is common place in older female dogs who are not spayed and have not had a litter of puppies. *If you don't use it, you lose it.* Muckwah needed an operation as soon as possible because her condition could be fatal. The operation was going to cost $1,650 dollars. Our dear friend Sharon made up a fundraiser on our public page for Muckwah. With Steve's help we set out to do daily fundraisers of our own. The response to help my baby girl was so fantastic that it actually made me cry. We had raised the money in only seven short days.

In another four days Muckwah would be getting her life saving surgery. The Vet even agreed to remove the lumps from her skin at no extra cost.

You have absolutely no idea of just how afraid I was for my beloved baby girl. After Steve dropped us off, Sharon and Kathy Knox agreed to pick us up later. Muck would not be able to walk on her own until the following day. I would need help getting her into the car and then up the stairs into Steve's house. *And yes, I never left the Vet's that entire time.*

Thank God Muckwahs surgery was a success. She would now

need to wear something to keep her from licking her stitches while she healed. Instead of a cone, our dear Sharon purchased a special after surgery dog shirt for Muckwah. The three of us had no problem getting Muckwah into the back seat of Sharon's car - all 140 lbs of her. But when it proved way too difficult to get her up the stairs at Steve's, our dear, dear sweet Sharon insisted that Muckwah and I spend the night in the back room of her shop. It was at ground level.

Muckwah recovering from surgery at Sharon's shop

Muckwah was still under the anesthetic they had used and wouldn't be out of it until morning. During one of our surgery fundraiser's on a Sunday and out front of the CIBC bank on Lacley . *The bank was closed on Sunday.* A very sweet girl who worked next door at the Lacley Pharmacy came out for a visit. She gave Muckwah her very own stuffed baby Husky. Muckwah loved it so much that I let her use it for a pillow the night we spent at Sharon's shop. In the morning I was so happy to see my baby girl wide awake and wanting to go for a walk. Sharon showed up shortly after to make sure that we were okay and I told her that I had already called Steve and that he was on his way to pick us up.

That first week after surgery, we just stayed around Steve's as I gradually walked Muck a little further each day, I was also able to get back to helping Jackie and Steve.

Before we continue, there are two very important things that happened during our surgery fundraiser's that I almost forgot to mention.

On our very first day of fundraising we decided to try our old spot at the Metro on Front Street. While there we had the most amazing surprise visit from our very dear old friend Carrie Cyr from Blind River.

Carrie had a sister in Bracebridge, which was two towns over from Washago. After her visit with her sister, Carrie wanted to make sure that she stopped to see us, just so it would be a surprise. Dear sweet Carrie had contacted Uncle Steve on messenger, gotten his phone number and called him when she was ready to come for her visit. Dear old Uncle Steve told them exactly where we were and didn't even bother to call me. *Thanks Steve, you sly old dog, you.* Well, as Muckwah and I were just sitting at Metro minding our own business this beautiful vintage 1965 Ford Mustang pulls into the parking space directly in front of us. As I was admiring this gorgeous machine, I didn't even notice the lady getting out on the passenger's side. At least not until she said: *"Hey there stranger."*

I looked up to see our dear friend Carrie. I noticed her husband Ron getting out the driver's side, followed by their three children, Wayne, Emma and Muckwah's personal favorite Karleigh. *WOW, Holy family reunion Batman!*

Just then our dear Uncle Steve pulled into the spot right beside them. We had the best visit ever where Karleigh spent most of her time just hugging and petting Muckwah and getting her face soaking wet from "Muck Kisses". It was just so sweet to see those two together again. It was almost like they had never been apart. Uncle Steve even managed to take a couple of group pictures of all of us.

Muck and I with our adopted family from Blind River

The second time was while we were at one of our two regular spots, Sobeys up in Gravenhurst. While we were fundraising we had a visit from a very sweet young girl and her Mom. Together they had been following our public page on Facebook. Between the two of them they had managed to raise $400 to put towards Muckwahs surgery. In return that sweet little girl got a whole heap of Muck kisses for her effort. She laughed and said that the kisses were well worth it.

The girl who donated $400 towards Mucks surgery

We now return you to your regularly scheduled reading.

While Muckwah was recovering, we were all doing our best to clean out the house for the sale. It was a little too much for the four of us. Steve's nephew Peter would come over with his trailer and do dump runs. Jackie and Steve decided to hire an auctioneer to help clean the place out. Well, wasn't I surprised when the auctioneer showed up that first day.

We both recognized each other right away. This guy was the spineless punk who had tried to start a fight with me the year before at the Independent grocery store in Gravenhurst, because he didn't like homeless people.

Muckwah and I had been doing a fundraiser at the Independent when this jerk in a Ford from the 90's parks in the firelane. He gets out, comes storming right up to me and tells me that he doesn't allow drug addicted homeless garbage to beg out front of his store.

My first response was: *"This is "Your" store, and you're driving that pile of crap, yeah right."* He came back with: *"If you don't leave right now,*

I'm gonna kick the living shit right out of you." Well, you should have seen the look on this punks face as I stood up and walked right over to him saying: *"Okay go ahead and kick the shit out of me!"*

The color just vanished from his face and his eyes went wide as he then stormed away and into the store yelling: *"I'm calling the cop's, you asshole!"* This jerk was exactly like most bullies, all mouth and absolutely no guts.

When he showed up at Steve's that day, I was sitting on the front porch having a smoke. This time he had five other guys with him - his work crew. As he walked up the steps and got near to me, he looked at me and said: *"Looks like you finally found somebody to sponge off of, so are you gonna get off your lazy no good homeless ass and help out or what."*

Not wanting to wreck anything for Steve, I just looked right at him and said: *"I don't take orders from you."*

After this lovely encounter I talked to Steve and we both agreed it was best that I just stayed out of the way while they were here. It would only be three times a week. It was Jackie's idea that we mark anything we didn't want them to take. My room was off limits to them. I *even padlocked my door when I wasn't there.* The only item of mine that was not in my room was the very large pet carrier I had borrowed to bring Muckwah down on the train. I also needed it to bring her back up north with me. I made up a very large sign that read *"Please Don't Take"* I then taped it in plain sight to the top of the carrier. Well didn't that punk order his guys to load it onto his truck anyway. *WTF?!*

As luck would have it, I just happened to be out in the kitchen getting Muckwah a fresh drink when I looked out the window overlooking Steve's driveway just in time to see his guys loading my pet carrier on to their truck. I flew out the front door, down the steps and got my carrier back. Even though it was a little crowded, I put the carrier in our room. Later when I told Steve what they tried to do, Steve told me that they said it wasn't marked. *Bullshit!*

We were now in to December and again Steve would be going to his sisters for Christmas. I wanted to do a furball Christmas just like the year before, but sadly Steve had lost his house cat Tommy to old age while we had been gone. This year it would only be me, Muckwah, Dalton and the fourteen feral cats - plus 3 raccoons I had made friends with. Even though I didn't drink anymore, I got a small bottle of Kahlua to share with Steve for New Year's Eve. I had two drinks and passed out.

The winter was real brutal that year with lots of snow. Because he didn't think he needed it anymore, Steve had given his snow blower to his nephew Peter for helping us out. *Big mistake!* That winter I shoveled the driveway as Steve did the steps and the front and back deck's.

We didn't do much fundraising until the weather let up in late February. I just spent my time shoveling snow, taking Muckwah for her walks, working on Book 2 and watching TV with Steve. We did however go into Orillia at least twice a week.

It was during one of our many shopping trips to Costco that we both had the most adorable puppy moments ever. This day the store was way more crowded than usual. We got our usual hotdogs amd for some reason Steve just had to get a butterscotch sundae. We couldn't find a seat anywhere, so we decided to eat out in the car. *Not a very good idea.*

I was sitting in the passenger's seat with my drink in my right hand and my hotdog in my left with my elbow on the center console. I was holding my hotdog straight up so nothing would leak out. As I took the first bite of my hotdog, to my surprise all I got was bun. I looked behind me, there was dear old Muckwah laying at the far back of the car enjoying my hotdog. Without me noticing or even feeling anything, Muckwah had snuck up behind me and stolen my dog right out of the bun. *Damn, she was good!*

Steve and I both cracked up laughing. After Steve finished his sundae, he passed the cup back to Dalton. He had left some in the bottom for Dalton. As we were about to pull out of the parking lot,

Dalton started crying and making a huge fuss from behind Steve. The poor little guy had actually gotten the cup stuck to his nose. Another really good bout of laughter followed.

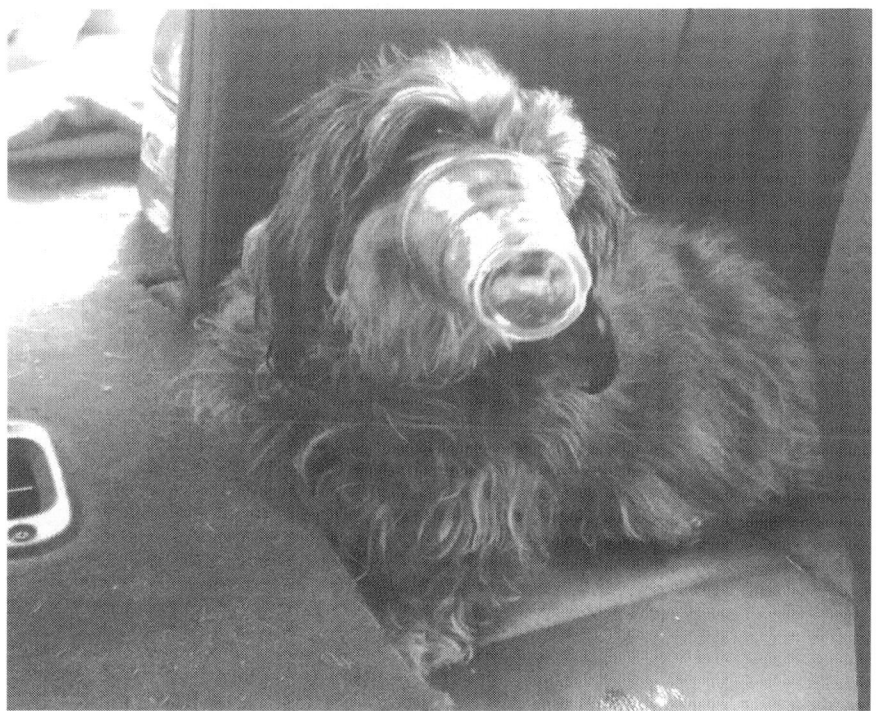

Dalton and Muckwah having fun at Costco's

After the weather had turned for the better and Steve and Dalton were back on a regular schedule of Paws Therapy three times a week, Muckwah and I were able to get back to our fundraisers. Once a week at Sobeys in Gravenhurst, twice a week at Food Basics on Coldwater and every Sunday in front of the CIBC on Lacley Ave.

Our dear friend Victor visited us from Mexico

During this winter we had made a new friend on Facebook by the name of Victor. Victor lived in Mexico, owned two Malamute's and we both belonged to the same Malamute group. Victor had even made an extremely large donation towards Muck's surgery!

It just so happened that Victor worked for a large company in Mexico that was expanding into Canada. They were opening their first office in Toronto and Victor would be coming up to oversee this operation. He asked me if he could come visit us while he was in Canada. It was only a three hour drive. I was way more than happy to welcome Victor over to Uncle Steve's.

Around the same time Muckwah and I had started a new tradition during our Sunday fundraisers at the CIBC. At the other end of the plaza was a really great restaurant called Friends Diner. These guys made the very best chili cheese dog on earth. I would get one for each of us every Sunday. Well it just happened to be a Sunday when Victor came up from Toronto to visit. I told him where we were, gave him directions and around twelve-thirty that afternoon Victor pulled his rental car in to the CIBC parking lot. We hadn't eaten yet and Victor offered to treat for lunch. When he asked me what I wanted for lunch I said: *"How about some KFC?"* Victor just started laughing as he said: *Who in their right mind eats that crap."*

Okay, Woody!

I asked him if he ever had a chili cheese dog. When he said no, well into Friends Diner we went. *Victor just loved it!* After lunch Victor drove us up to Washago where I introduced him to our dear Uncle Steve and Dalton. We all had a great visit that lasted at least two hours. We took a few pictures and then sadly Victor had to head back to Toronto. He had work in the morning. Muckwah just loved Victor.

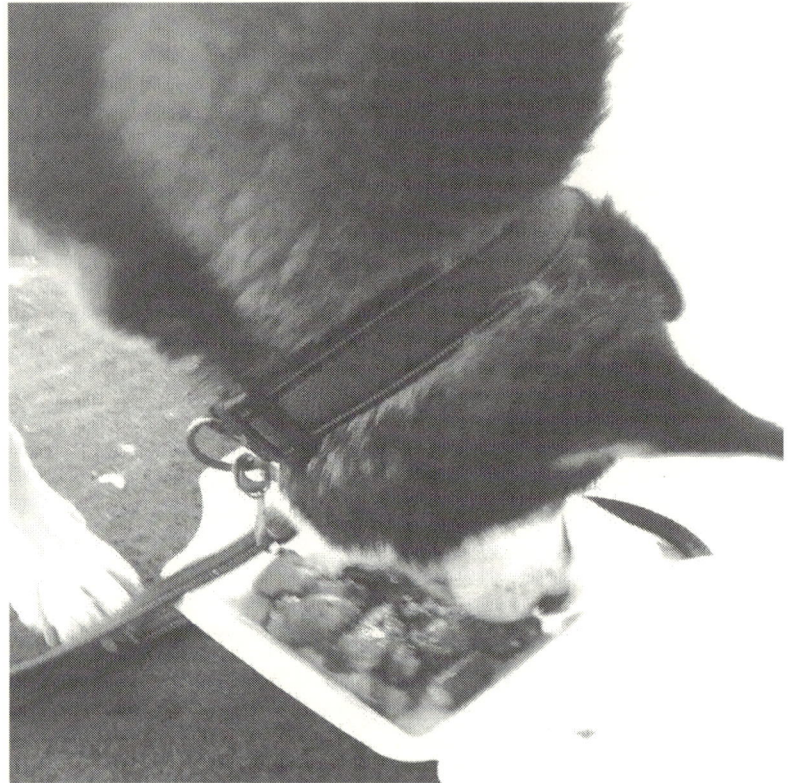

Muckwah enjoying her chili cheese dog from Friends Diner

It wasn't until the second week of March that Steve and I both started noticing a little bit of strange behavior in Muckwah.

This started just the odd time as she was walking through the house, she seemed to lose her balance just a little. Then a week later she was starting to have difficulty climbing the stairs into Steve's house. During the final week of March, my poor baby girl was even having a hard time getting up in Steve's car. That was when I got really scared and made an appointment with the vet.

Our appointment was for Wednesday April 3 at 1 o'clock in the afternoon. I wanted to go for our regular Sunday fundraiser because we really needed the money to pay for the vet's appointment.

On Sunday morning March 31, Steve picked us up at his house at 10:50 am. Just as we were about to get on the highway going to

Orillia, Muckwah started having a fit from the back of the car. She was having difficulty breathing. Thinking that she might be choking on something I yelled at Steve to pull over and stop the car. I jumped out and ripped open the back door to check on her.

On Sunday morning at eleven o'clock, the Greatest Love of my entire life, my Beloved Baby Girl Muckwah died in my Arms. I had just been struck by the greatest tragedy of my entire life.

Trying his best to comfort me but having absolutely no success - I just couldn't stop crying, not even for a second - Steve got on his phone, called Sharon and told her what just happened. Even though it was Sunday and she was closed, Sharon told Steve to bring us and meet her at her shop in Orillia. Sharon owned a business called Pets at Peace North. It was a Pet Funeral Parlor and grief counseling. Without hesitating Sharon just dropped whatever she had been doing to come help us. *I really, really love that woman!*

Our dear sweet sharon said that she would take the best care she could with my baby girl, and not to worry Muckwah was in very good hands. *I already knew that.* As I said my final goodbye to the Greatest Love of my Entire Life, I made Muckwah a solemn promise that no matter what it took, I would somehow find a way to finish what we started, or I would die trying. By God I meant every single word of my promise.

Finally we were on our way back to Washago with me now crying uncontrollably. Poor heartbroken Steve beside me trying everything he could to console me. Unable to stop my tears, not even enough to talk to poor Steve I just went to my room where the worst day of my life eventually turned into the worst night of my life.

The one thing I was feeling more than the loss of my beloved baby girl, was just plain lost. At that moment in my life I saw absolutely nothing in front of me. *Just a big black emptiness.*

Muckwah and I had gone through hell and back, struggling for two and a half years to make a name for ourselves. I now found myself questioning just who Homeless James could possibly be without his Muckwah. All I could come up with was *nothing*!

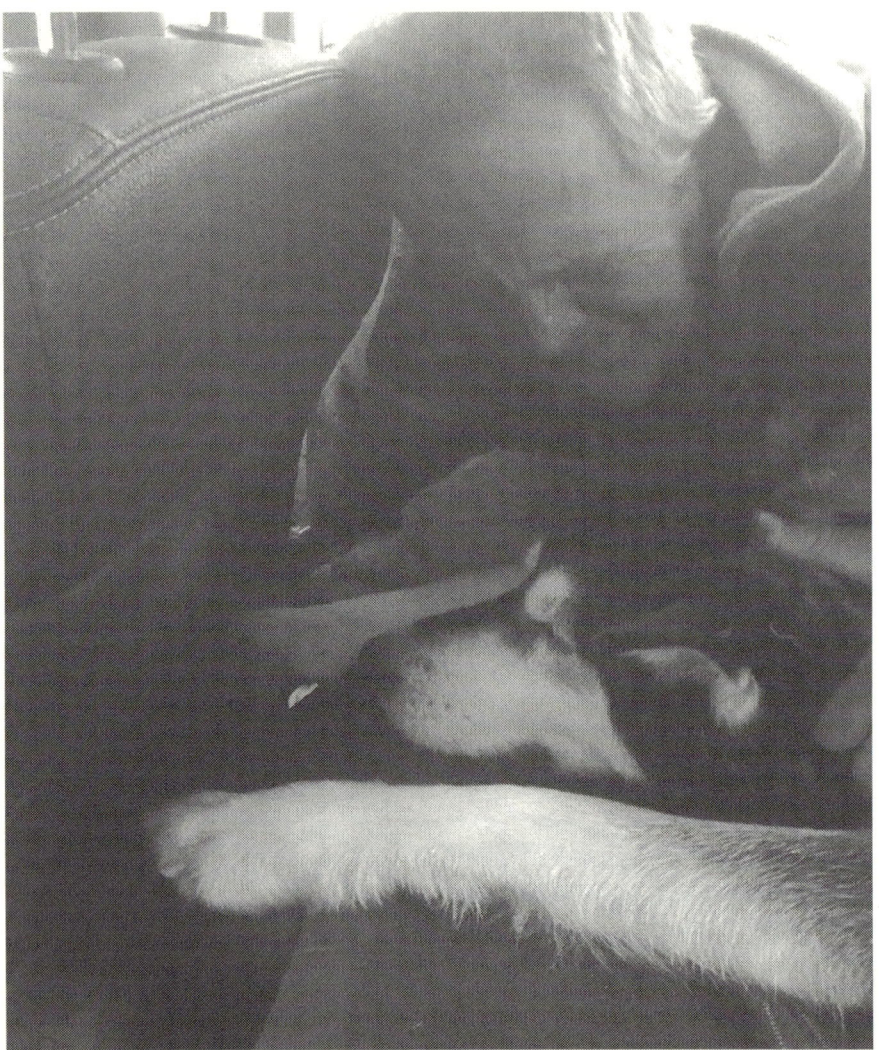

The most tragic day of my entire life. I asked Sharon to take a picture of me saying Goodbye

I eventually cried myself to sleep around four in the morning. I woke up at nine o'clock praying to God that it was just a bad dream. *It wasn't.* I slowly shuffled out to the kitchen to get my morning coffee. When Steve saw me he told me not to bother and to get dressed because he was taking me into town for breakfast.

82

I told him that I didn't feel up to it, he insisted and even kept at me until I agreed. He took me to A&W for my favorite breakfast, and on our way home to my unwanted surprise.

Steve pulled his car into the parking lot of the Orillia SPCA. Unknown to me Steve had also been up all night checking pet adoption sites on the internet. He had found what he thought was the perfect match for me right here in Orillia. *Sneaky old fart now, wasn't he.*

Without letting on Steve insisted that I come in with him to see what they had. *Did I ever mention just how much I love that sneaky old fart?*

I opened the door to the kennels I automatically looked to my left. As God is my witness, my heart must have skipped a beat and it felt exactly like being hit by lightning.

Just six feet in front of me was the most adorable Siberian Husky I had ever seen. He even had a face almost identical to Muckwah. At that very instant I just knew in my heart that this was Divine Intervention.

It was pure love at first sight and thanks to God, Steve and Muckwah, I would not be alone. Our walk would now continue and my heart would eventually heal. As I went back out to the desk, with Steve's help the girl there already had the paperwork filled out. *WOW!*

I just needed to pay the $450 adoption fee and Banjo would be all mine.

Not having the money, I went out for a smoke while I made a post on our public Facebook page explaining how I had lost Muckwah and the situation I now found myself in.

Exactly ten minutes after making that post I got a response from a wonderful woman out in Rama telling me to just stay exactly where I was. She was already in her car and on her way into Orillia. When she got there she paid the fee and asked me if she could please remain anonymous. I told her no problem.

Now the way everything just happened, I double dog dare anyone out there to tell me that this was not Divine Intervention! As we drove back to Steve's with my new best buddy, my heart was still broken, but I now had something I didn't have when I woke up this morning.

Not only did I now have a new best friend, I now had something called Hope.

HOW CAN YOU HELP?

Fundraising along the road can sometimes be challenging, so another way that you can support them is via e-mail money transfer. Please send donations can be sent to jamesandmuck@hotmail.com. The account is set up as open deposit so no security question is required.

You can help James and Muckwah on their journey by purchasing copies of this book. Don't forget to purchase a few copies for friends and family as well.

Help by spreading the word – tell everyone you know about this amazing story. Got media connections? Let them know too! Every bit of publicity that we can get helps!

Other ways to help?

Support the local homeless shelters in your area; lobby your local government and communities to create and support homeless shelters that allow companion animals.

Manufactured by Amazon.ca
Bolton, ON

28541853R00055